California
Cookbook

Authentic California Cooking with Easy California Recipes

By
BookSumo Press

Published by
http://www.booksumo.com

Table of Contents

Corn Cakes California 26

American Corn Dogs 27

Curried Spinach with Chicken 28

California Mock Cake Pops 29

Mixed Green Salad with Onion Vinaigrette 30

California Tofu Breakfast Skillet 31

Sunshine Pineapple Cake 32

Sunshine Muffins 33

Glendale Grocery Rotisserie Dip 34

Barley Bean Sprout Boxes 35

Cupertino Cashews Chickpeas 36

California Shrimp Bowls 37

3 Cheese Quesadilla 38

Pasadena Polenta Salad 39

Anaheim Corn Pizza 40

Calabasas Casserole 41

Monterey Artichoke Quesadillas 42

Mexican Meringue Squares 43

California Cucumbers with Dill Vinaigrette 44

Spicy Cheese & Walnut Log 45

Bread Mountain View 46

Sonoma Potato Salad 91

Moor park Seafood Au Gratin Dip 92

American Ground Beef Casserole 93

Pasta Salad California 94

Los Angeles Monterey Quiche 95

California
Focaccia Sandwich

🥣 Prep Time: 30 mins
🕐 Total Time: 50 mins

Servings per Recipe: 4
Calories	203.2
Fat	15.9g
Cholesterol	20.5mg
Sodium	321.5mg
Carbohydrates	11.9g
Protein	4.3g

Ingredients

1/4 C. mayonnaise
3 garlic cloves, minced
1 tbsp lemon juice
1/8 C. olive oil
1 C. sliced red bell pepper
1 small zucchini, sliced
1 red onion, sliced

1 small yellow squash, sliced
focaccia bread
1/2 C. crumbled feta cheese

Directions

1. In a bowl, mix together the mayonnaise, garlic and lemon juice.
2. Refrigerate before using.
3. Set your grill for high heat and grease the grill grate.
4. Coat the vegetables with olive oil evenly.
5. Place the zucchini and bell peppers closest to the middle of the grill and arrange the squash and onion pieces around them.
6. Cook for about 3 minutes, per side.
7. Remove from the grill and keep aside.
8. Spread some of the mayonnaise mixture on the cut sides of the bread and sprinkle each one with feta cheese.
9. Place the bread pieces on the grill, cheese side up and cover with lid for about 2-3 minutes.
10. Remove from the grill and top with the vegetables.
11. Serve immediately.

BAJA
Bean Dip

Prep Time: 15 mins
Total Time: 8 hrs 15 mins

Servings per Recipe: 32
Calories   100.7
Fat   5.3g
Cholesterol   2.0mg
Sodium   140.4mg
Carbohydrates   11.0g
Protein   3.1g

Ingredients

2 (11 oz.) cans white corn, drained
2 (15 oz.) cans black beans, rinsed and drained
1/2 C. Italian salad dressing
1 C. ranch salad dressing
1 small onion, chopped
1 tsp hot pepper sauce

2 tsp cilantro, chopped fresh
1 tsp chili powder
1/2 tsp ground black pepper

Directions

1. In a bowl, add all the ingredients and mix until well combined.
2. Refrigerate, covered to chill for about 8 hours or overnight before serving.

Baja Style
Gravy

 Prep Time: 10 mins

Total Time: 20 mins

Servings per Recipe: 6
Calories	43.9
Fat	2.4g
Cholesterol	0.0mg
Sodium	506.6mg
Carbohydrates	4.1g
Protein	2.1g

Ingredients

1 tbsp vegetable oil
1/2 lb. mushroom, sliced
3 tbsp tamari soy sauce
ground black pepper

1 1/2 C. hot water
2 tbsp cornstarch, dissolved in 1/2 C. water

Directions

1. In a skillet, heat the oil and sauté the mushrooms, tamari and black pepper until mushrooms are tender.
2. Stir in the water and bring to a boil.
3. Slowly, add the cornstarch and simmer until gravy is thick, stirring continuously.
4. Serve hot.

HERMOSA
Hummus Sandwiches

Prep Time: 10 mins
Total Time: 10 mins

Servings per Recipe: 1

Calories	780.4
Fat	38.9g
Cholesterol	0.0mg
Sodium	722.3mg
Carbohydrates	94.0g
Protein	23.6g

Ingredients

1/2 C. cooked quinoa, cooled
1/3 C. hummus
1 small avocado, sliced
2 tsp lemon juice
salt and pepper

3 slices sandwich bread
1 roma tomato, sliced
1 C. quinoa mixed sprouts

Directions

1. In small bowl, mix together the quinoa and hummus.
2. In another bowl, add the avocado, lemon juice, salt and pepper and toss to coat well.
3. Spread the quinoa mixture on one side of each bread slice and top one slice with the avocado, followed by the tomato and sprouts.
4. Cover with remaining bread slice.
5. Repeat the layers.
6. Cut the sandwich in half and serve.

Gonzales
Garlic Bread

Prep Time: 15 mins
Total Time: 3 hrs 15 mins

Servings per Recipe: 8
Calories	274.8
Fat	4.1g
Cholesterol	0.0mg
Sodium	575.0mg
Carbohydrates	52.0g
Protein	7.1g

Ingredients

1 1/2 C. tomato vegetable juice,
1/3 C. snipped sun-dried tomato
3 cloves roasted garlic
1 1/2 tsp salt
2 tbsp sugar
2 tbsp extra-virgin olive oil

3 3/4 C. bread flour
1 tbsp dried basil
1 3/4 tsp bread machine yeast

Directions

1. In a bread machine pan, add all the ingredients in the order recommended by the manufacturer.
2. Select Basic Cycle and press the Start.
3. When the baking cycle is completed, immediately remove the bread from the pan and place onto a wire rack to cool before slicing.

PACIFIC
Orange Salad

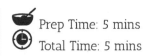 Prep Time: 5 mins
Total Time: 5 mins

Servings per Recipe: 4
Calories   279.0
Fat   20.0g
Cholesterol   0.0mg
Sodium   29.3mg
Carbohydrates   26.6g
Protein   4.5g

Ingredients

10 oz. salad greens
15 oz. mandarin oranges, canned
1/4 C. red onion, sliced
1/4 C. pecans, toasted
1/2 C. balsamic vinaigrette

2 avocados, seeded, peeled and chopped

Directions

1. In a large bowl, mix together the salad greens, red onion, oranges and pecans.
2. In a small bowl, add the vinaigrette and 1/2 C. of the avocado and with a fork, mix the avocado into the dressing.
3. Add the remaining avocado and t dressing into the salad and toss to coat well.
4. Serve immediately.

Granny Smith Cake

🥣 Prep Time: 40 mins
🕐 Total Time: 1 hr 30 mins

Servings per Recipe: 12
Calories   373.7
Fat   16.0g
Cholesterol   35.2mg
Sodium   492.5mg
Carbohydrates   54.1g
Protein   5.3g

Ingredients

4 C. peeled and sliced apples
1 3/4 C. sugar
1/2 C. oil
1 C. chopped walnuts
2 eggs, well beaten
2 tsp vanilla
2 C. flour

2 tsp baking soda
2 tsp cinnamon
1 tsp salt

Directions

1. Set your oven to 350 degrees F before doing anything else and grease a 13x9-inch baking dish.
2. Ina bowl, mix together the flour, baking soda, cinnamon and salt.
3. In a large bowl, add the apples and sugar and mix well.
4. Add the eggs, nuts, oil and vanilla and mix well.
5. Add the flour mixture and mix until well combined.
6. Place the mixture into prepared baking dish evenly.
7. Cook in the oven for about 50-60 minutes.
8. Remove from the oven and keep onto the wire rack to cool in the pan for about 10 minutes.
9. Carefully, invert the cake onto the wire rack to cool completely before serving.

CHULA
Vista Crab Melt

 Prep Time: 20 mins
Total Time: 23 mins

Servings per Recipe: 4
Calories	1188.5
Fat	31.6g
Cholesterol	73.4mg
Sodium	2744.3mg
Carbohydrates	171.4g
Protein	50.2g

Ingredients

1 (8 oz.) packet crab meat, chopped
1/2 C. light mayonnaise
1/4 C. green onion, sliced
6 oz. Swiss cheese, shredded
1/2 tsp garlic salt

1/4 tsp paprika
20 slices sourdough bread

Directions

1. Set the broiler of your oven and arrange oven rack about 5-6-inch from the heating element.
2. In a bowl, add all the ingredients except bread and mix until well combined.
3. Arrange the bread slices onto a large baking sheet.
4. Cook under the broiler for about 1-2 minutes.
5. Flip the bread slices and top each with the crab meat mixture evenly.
6. Cook under the broiler for about 23 minutes.
7. Serve immediately.

40 Minute
California Dinner

Prep Time: 10 mins
Total Time: 40 mins

Servings per Recipe: 4
Calories   647.4
Fat   49.6g
Cholesterol   14.8mg
Sodium   643.5mg
Carbohydrates   39.5g
Protein   18.5g

Ingredients

3 C. diced cooked chicken
2 C. slivered almonds
1/4 C. chopped pimiento
1 1/2 C. mayonnaise
3 tbsp lemon juice
3 tbsp grated onions
1/2 tsp salt

1/2 tsp pepper
1 packet frozen baby peas, cooked
1 C. crushed potato chips
1/2 C. grated cheddar cheese

Directions

1. Set your oven to 350 degrees F before doing anything else and grease a casserole dish.
2. In a large bowl, add all the ingredients except the potato chips and cheese and mix well.
3. Place the mixture into the prepared casserole dish evenly and top with the potato chips and grated cheese.
4. Cook in the oven for about 30-0 minutes.

CHICKEN
& Rice California

Prep Time: 15 mins
Total Time: 1 hr 5 mins

Servings per Recipe: 4
Calories	650.9
Fat	13.9g
Cholesterol	92.8mg
Sodium	542.3mg
Carbohydrates	93.8g
Protein	35.9g

Ingredients

4 chicken breasts, boneless and skinless
1 small onion, chopped
1/2 C. brown sugar
1/2 C. ketchup
1/4 C. chunky salsa
1/8 tsp cayenne pepper
1/8 tsp seasoning mix

1 1/2 C. white rice
3 C. water
1 (500 g) packet frozen vegetables
1/8 tsp rosemary
1/8 tsp fresh ground pepper
butter

Directions

1. Set your oven to 350 degrees F before doing anything else.
2. In a small bowl, mix together the onion, ketchup, salsa, brown sugar and spices.
3. In a rectangular baking dish, place the chicken breasts and top with the salsa mixture.
4. In an oven-safe pan, mix together the rice and water.
5. Cook the chicken and rice in the oven for about 30 minutes.
6. Meanwhile, in a medium microwave-safe casserole dish, place the vegetables and microwave, covered on high for about 5 minutes.
7. Remove from the microwave and stir in the spices.
8. Microwave on High for about 2 minutes.
9. Add the butter and stir to combine.
10. Serve the chicken alongside the rice and vegetables.

Monica's
Fish Cakes

🥣 Prep Time: 15 mins
🕐 Total Time: 21 mins

Servings per Recipe: 6
Calories	319.2
Fat	14.3g
Cholesterol	44.9mg
Sodium	683.5mg
Carbohydrates	25.3g
Protein	21.2g

Ingredients

1 (6 oz.) packet seasoned stuffing mix
3/4 C. water
1/3 C. mayonnaise
2 (6 oz.) cans tuna, drained and flaked
1 tbsp lemon juice

1 C. cheddar cheese, shredded
1 green onion, chopped
tartar sauce

Directions

1. In a bowl, add all the ingredients and mix until well combined.
2. Refrigerate, covered for about 10 minutes.
3. With 1/3 C. of the tuna mixture, make patties.
4. Heat a greased large nonstick skillet over medium heat and cook the patties for about 3 minutes per side.
5. Served alongside the tartar sauce.

CHOCOLATE
Cookie Balls

Prep Time: 10 mins
Total Time: 20 mins

Servings per Recipe: 1
Calories	82.4
Fat	4.5g
Cholesterol	3.7mg
Sodium	34.7mg
Carbohydrates	10.1g
Protein	1.3g

Ingredients

2 oz. unsweetened chocolate squares
1 (14 oz.) cans sweetened condensed milk
3 C. sweetened flaked coconut

1 tsp vanilla extract
36 whole blanched almonds

Directions

1. Set your oven to 350 degrees F before doing anything else and line a baking sheet with a lightly greased parchment paper.
2. In a microwave-safe bowl, add the chocolate and sweetened condensed milk and microwave until melted and smooth, stirring after every 1 minute.
3. In a large bowl, add the chocolate mixture, coconut and vanilla and mix until well combined.
4. With a teaspoon, place the mixture onto the prepared baking sheet and top each cookie with an almond, pressing down slightly.
5. Cook in the oven for about 12 minutes.
6. Remove from the oven and keep onto the wire rack to cool in the pan for about 5 minutes.
7. Carefully, invert the cookies onto the wire rack to cool completely.

Peanut Chicken With Fruity Salsa

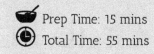

Prep Time: 15 mins
Total Time: 55 mins

Servings per Recipe: 6
Calories	386.0
Fat	23.4g
Cholesterol	115.2mg
Sodium	955.9mg
Carbohydrates	10.1g
Protein	34.5g

Ingredients

12 skinless chicken thighs
1/2 C. hot water
1/2 C. creamy peanut butter
1/4 C. chili sauce
1/4 C. soy sauce
2 tbsp vegetable oil
2 tbsp vinegar
4 cloves garlic, minced
2 tsp grated ginger root
1/4 tsp cayenne pepper

1 C. chopped fresh fruit (peaches, plums, pears, apricots etc.)
1 C. seeded chopped cucumber
2 tbsp thinly sliced green onions
2 tbsp snipped cilantro
1 tbsp sugar
1 tbsp vegetable oil
1 tbsp vinegar

Directions

1. Rinse the chicken well and with the paper towels, pat dry.
2. In large bowl, add the peanut butter and slowly, add the hot water, stirring continuously until smooth.
3. Stir in soy sauce, chili sauce, 2 tbsp of the oil, the 2 tbsp of the vinegar, ginger, garlic and cayenne until well combined. Add the chicken and coat with mixture generously.
4. Refrigerator for about 12-24 hours, flipping occasionally. In a bowl, mix together the chopped fruit, cucumber, green onion, cilantro, sugar, and 1 tbsp of the vinegar and 1 tbsp of the oil. Refrigerate, covered to chill for about 1 hour.
5. Set the broiler of your oven and arrange oven rack about 8-inch from the heating element. Remove chicken from the bowl and discard the marinade. Cook under the broiler for about 15 minutes, flipping occasionally. Now, set the oven to 350 degrees F.
6. Cook the chicken in oven for about 25 minutes.
7. Serve the chicken with the topping of the salsa.

PLUM TOMATO
& Crab Pizza

Prep Time: 10 mins
Total Time: 25 mins

Servings per Recipe: 10
Calories	206.1
Fat	12.3g
Cholesterol	26.8mg
Sodium	406.1mg
Carbohydrates	17.5g
Protein	7.5g

Ingredients

1 (8 oz.) packet dinner rolls
2 ripe avocados, peeled and mashed
2 tbsp onions, finely chopped
1 tbsp lemon juice
1/4 C. sour cream
1/2 tsp salt
4 oz. Monterey jack cheese, shredded

4 oz. imitation crab meat, chopped
2 plum tomatoes, seeded and chopped
2 tbsp cilantro

Directions

1. Set your oven to 350 degrees F before doing anything else.
2. Unroll the crescent dough and separate into 8 triangles.
3. Arrange the dough triangles onto a round baking stone in a circle with points in the center and wide ends toward the outside.
4. With a lightly floured rolling pin, roll out dough to a 12-inch circle, pressing seams together to seal.
5. Cook in the oven for about 12-15 minutes.
6. Remove from the oven and keep aside to cool completely.
7. In a bowl, mix together the sour cream, avocado, onion, lemon juice and salt.
8. Spread avocado mixture over the crust evenly and top with the cheese, followed by crab meat, tomato and cilantro.
9. Cut into squares and serve.

Folsom
Rice Bowls

🥣 Prep Time: 15 mins

🕐 Total Time: 30 mins

Servings per Recipe: 8

Calories	223.2
Fat	14.3g
Cholesterol	0.0mg
Sodium	334.4mg
Carbohydrates	22.0g
Protein	2.4g

Ingredients

1 C. basmati rice

6 radishes, halved and sliced

1/2 C. red bell pepper, diced

1/2 C. red onion, diced

2 beets, cooked, peeled, and diced

1/4 C. fresh scallions, chopped

2 tbsp fresh dill, chopped

Vinaigrette

1/4 C. white vinegar

1 1/2 tbsp prepared horseradish

1 tbsp whole grain mustard

1-2 tsp sugar

1 tsp salt

fresh ground black pepper

1/2 C. extra virgin olive oil

Directions

1. Cook the rice according to package's directions.
2. Keep side to cool.
3. In a large bowl, mix together the rice, bell pepper, beets, radishes, red onion, chives and dill.
4. For the dressing: in a bowl, add all the ingredients and beat whisking until smooth.
5. Pour the dressing over the rice mixture and toss to coat well.
6. Serve immediately.

CHINO'S
Chili

Prep Time: 20 mins
Total Time: 1 hr 20 mins

Servings per Recipe: 6
Calories   1500.5
Fat   113.3g
Cholesterol   149.8mg
Sodium   542.6mg
Carbohydrates   86.5g
Protein   39.7g

Ingredients

2-4 lb. beef, cubed
1-2 tbsp oil
3-8 garlic cloves
1 large onion, chopped
4 tbsp chili powder
3 tsp cayenne pepper
3 tsp chili pepper flakes
3 tbsp cumin
2 tsp paprika
2 tbsp white pepper
3 tbsp dried cilantro

4 tbsp dried parsley
1 cans tomatoes, chopped
2 cans green chilies, roasted
1 cans chili beans
1 cans kidney beans
1 cans pinto bean
1 cans black beans

Directions

1. In large Dutch oven, heat the oil and cook the beef, onion and garlic until medium brown.
2. Stir in the cumin, chili powder, cayenne pepper, pepper flakes and White pepper and cook until browned completely.
3. Add the tomatoes, chilies, beans and dried herbs and stir to combine.
4. Reduce the heat to medium-low and simmer for about 1 1/2 hours.
5. Serve with your desired topping.

Crispy
Tofu

🥣 Prep Time: 10 mins
🕐 Total Time: 30 mins

Servings per Recipe: 4
Calories   313.5
Fat   5.8g
Cholesterol   47.2mg
Sodium   264.9mg
Carbohydrates   50.5g
Protein   15.0g

Ingredients

1 lb. extra-soft tofu, pressed and drained
2 C. all-purpose flour
1 tsp seasoning salt
1/2 tsp garlic powder
1 tbsp soy sauce
1/2 tsp black pepper

1 egg yolk, slightly beaten
1 C. ice cold water
peanut oil
hoisin sauce, for dipping

Directions

1. In a shallow late, mix together 1 C. of the flour, seasoning salt, garlic powder and pepper.
2. In another shallow bowl, add the icy cold water, egg yolk, soy sauce and 1 C. of the flour and mix until just combined.
3. Cut the tofu into 1x1-inch squares.
4. Coat the tofu into the dry flour mixture and then dip into wet flour mixture evenly, shaking off the excess.
5. In a pan, add about 3-inch of the oil and heat to 350 degrees F and fry the tofu pieces until golden brown.
6. Transfer the tofu pieces onto paper towels-lined plate to drain.
7. Serve alongside the hoisin sauce.

CORN CAKES
California

Prep Time: 10 mins
Total Time: 30 mins

Servings per Recipe: 4
Calories   528.8
Fat   18.5g
Cholesterol   108.2mg
Sodium   709.7mg
Carbohydrates   77.8g
Protein   16.9g

Ingredients

2 tbsp olive oil
1 C. onion, diced
1 C. all-purpose flour
1 C. fine yellow cornmeal
1 tsp salt
2 C. frozen corn, thawed

2 C. finely chopped kale
2 large eggs
2 tbsp olive oil
2 C. nonfat milk

Directions

1. In a large non-stick skillet, heat 1-2 tbsp of the olive oil and sauté the onion until golden.
2. In a large bowl, mix together the flour, cornmeal, corn, kale and salt.
3. In another bowl, add the eggs, milk and 2 tbsp of the olive oil and beat slightly.
4. Add the egg mixture into flour mixture and mix briefly.
5. Add the sautéed onion and mix well.
6. Heat the same pan with any remaining oil.
7. Place about 1/4 C. of the mixture and cook for about 3-5 minutes.
8. Flip and cook until golden from the other side.
9. Serve warm.

American
Corn Dogs

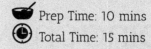 Prep Time: 10 mins
Total Time: 15 mins

Servings per Recipe: 10
Calories   1718.0
Fat   175.8g
Cholesterol   38.6mg
Sodium   560.2mg
Carbohydrates   35.9g
Protein   4.9g

Ingredients

1 3/4 C. flour
3/4 C. yellow cornmeal
1/2 C. sugar
1 3/4 tsp salt
1 tsp baking soda
1 3/4 C. nonfat milk

2 egg yolks, beaten
10 turkey hot dogs
8-10 C. vegetable oil
5 pairs of wooden chop sticks

Directions

1. In a large bowl, mix together the flour, corn meal, sugar, baking soda and salt.
2. In another bowl, add the milk and egg yolks and beat well.
3. Add the milk mixture into flour mixture and with an electric mixer beat on high speed until well combined and smooth.
4. With paper towels, pat dry the hot dogs and stick the thin end of a chopstick half way into each hot dog.
5. Coat the hot dogs with the milk mixture evenly.
6. In a deep fryer, heat the oil to 375 degrees F and fry the hot dogs in batches for about 5 minutes, turning with forks to evenly brown.
7. Transfer the hot dogs onto paper towels-lined plate to drain.

CURRIED
Spinach with Chicken

Prep Time: 30 mins
Total Time: 1 hr

Servings per Recipe: 4

Calories	287.7
Fat	17.7g
Cholesterol	63.6mg
Sodium	722.4mg
Carbohydrates	14.4g
Protein	19.3g

Ingredients

1 1/2 C. yogurt, divided
1 tbsp cornstarch
1/2 C. water
1 tsp salt
1 tbsp vegetable oil
1 onion, diced

1 (8 oz.) boxes frozen spinach, thawed and drained
2 tbsp curry powder
1-3 hot red pepper, chopped
1 lb. chicken

Directions

1. In a pan, heat the oil and cook the chicken until browned.
2. Transfer the chicken into a bowl.
3. In the same pan, add the onions and salt over medium heat and cook for about 3 minutes.
4. Add the curry powder and 1/2 C. of the yogurt and stir to combine.
5. Increase the heat to high and cook until fragrant.
6. Reduce heat to medium-high.
7. Stir in the red peppers and cook for about 1 minute.
8. Stir in the spinach and cook until warm.
9. In a bowl, dissolve the cornstarch in water.
10. Add corn starch slurry into the pan, stirring continuously until thickened.
11. Reduce heat to low and stir in the remaining yogurt and seasoning.
12. Remove from the heat and serve hot.

California
Mock Cake Pops

🥣 Prep Time: 1 hr
🕐 Total Time: 1 hr 20 mins

Servings per Recipe: 12
Calories	367.9
Fat	21.4g
Cholesterol	40.6mg
Sodium	186.0mg
Carbohydrates	40.8g
Protein	4.2g

Ingredients

1 C. butter
3 tbsp powdered sugar
2 C. flour, sifted
1 C. nuts, finely chopped

1 tbsp vanilla
2 C. powdered sugar

Directions

1. Set your oven to 350 degrees F before doing anything else.
2. In a bowl, add the butter and 3 tbsp of the powdered sugar and beat until creamy.
3. Add the vanilla and stir to combine.
4. Add the flour and nuts and mix until just combined.
5. Make tiny balls from the dough and arrange onto a cookie sheet.
6. Cook in the oven for about 20 minutes.
7. Remove from the oven and coat the hot cookies with the reserved powdered sugar.
8. Place the cookies onto wire rack to cool.
9. Coat the cookies with the powdered sugar again and serve.

MIXED
Green Salad with Onion Vinaigrette

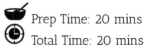

Prep Time: 20 mins
Total Time: 20 mins

Servings per Recipe: 6
Calories	321.8
Fat	28.2g
Cholesterol	0.0mg
Sodium	200.2mg
Carbohydrates	18.5g
Protein	2.1g

Ingredients

Onion Vinaigrette
1 tbsp yellow onion, chopped
2 tbsp cider vinegar
2 1/2 tbsp sugar
1/2 tsp dry mustard
1/2 tsp salt
1/2 tsp paprika
1 1/2 tsp celery seeds
1/2 C. vegetable oil

Salad
8 C. mixed salad greens, torn
1 sweet onion
2 avocados
2 fresh oranges

Directions

1. For the dressing: in a food processor, add all the ingredients and pulse until well combined.
2. Refrigerator before using.
3. For the salad: in a large salad bowl, place the greens.
4. Cut the onion into thin slices and separate into rings.
5. Peel, pit and slice the avocados.
6. Peel oranges and cut into bite sized pieces.
7. In the bowl of the greens, add the onion, avocados and orange and toss to coat.
8. Add the dressing and toss again.
9. Serve immediately.

California Tofu Breakfast Skillet

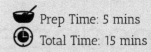

Prep Time: 5 mins
Total Time: 15 mins

Servings per Recipe: 1
Calories	188.1
Fat	11.5g
Cholesterol	0.0mg
Sodium	70.0mg
Carbohydrates	16.6g
Protein	9.8g

Ingredients

1/4 medium onion, diced
1/4 zucchini, diced
1/4 red sweet bell pepper, diced
2-4 garlic cloves, minced
1/2 small green chili pepper, diced
1-2 tsp olive oil
100 g tofu
1-2 tbsp canned spinach, chopped
1 tbsp vegan egg powder
1 tbsp fresh cilantro
1-1 1/2 tsp ground cumin
1-1 1/2 tsp dried oregano
1-1 1/2 tsp paprika
1 tsp dried parsley
1/2 tsp turmeric
1-2 lime wedge
soy sauce
fresh ground black pepper
1 green onion, chopped
1 tbsp avocado, diced

Directions

1. In a bowl, add the tofu, spinach, egg powder, cilantro and dried spices and with a fork, mash until well combined.

2. In a skillet, heat the oil over medium heat and cook the onion, zucchini, pepper, garlic and chile until onion is translucence.

3. Add the juice from the lime wedges and stir to combine.

4. Add the tofu mash and stir to combine.

5. Reduce the heat slightly and fry until heated through and well combined.

6. Stir in the soy sauce and black pepper and remove from the heat.

7. Serve with a garnishing of the green onion and avocado.

SUNSHINE
Pineapple Cake

Prep Time: 15 mins
Total Time: 1 hr 5 mins

Servings per Recipe: 10
Calories	376.6
Fat	17.2g
Cholesterol	69.5mg
Sodium	372.0mg
Carbohydrates	51.7g
Protein	4.6g

Ingredients

1 (18 1/2 oz.) packages yellow cake mix
3 eggs
1/3 C. oil
1 C. crushed pineapple
1/2 C. sour cream

Topping
1 tbsp crushed pineapple
1/2 C. sifted powdered sugar

Directions

1. Set your oven to 350 degrees F before doing anything else and grease a 10-inch tube pan
2. For the cake: in a bowl, add all the ingredients and with an electric mixer, beat on medium speed for about 4 minutes.
3. Place the mixture into the prepared tube pan evenly.
4. Cook in the oven for about 45-50 minutes or till a toothpick inserted in the center comes out clean.
5. Remove from the oven and keep onto the wire rack to cool in the pan for about 10 minutes.
6. Meanwhile, for the glaze, in a bowl, mix together the pineapple and sugar well.
7. Carefully, invert the cake onto the wire rack and pour the glaze on top.

Sunshine Muffins

Prep Time: 15 mins
Total Time: 35 mins

Servings per Recipe: 1
Calories	208.3
Fat	8.2g
Cholesterol	35.8mg
Sodium	306.1mg
Carbohydrates	32.0g
Protein	2.5g

Ingredients

1 large whole organic orange, washed and unpeeled
1/2 C. orange juice
1/2 C. chopped dates
1 large egg
1/2 C. butter, cut up
1 1/2 C. all-purpose flour
1 tsp baking soda
1 tsp baking powder
3/4 C. sugar
1/2 tsp salt

Directions

1. Set your oven to 400 degrees F before doing anything else and line the muffin pans with paper liners.
2. Cut orange into chunks and remove the seeds.
3. In a food processor, add the orange chunks and pulse until finely chopped.
4. Add the dates, orange juice, egg and butter and pulse until well combined.
5. In a bowl, mix together the flour, sugar, baking powder, baking soda and salt.
6. Add the orange mixture and stir until well combined.
7. Transfer the mixture into the prepared muffin cups about 3/4 full.
8. Cook in the oven for about 15-18 minutes or till a toothpick inserted in the center comes out clean.
9. Remove from the oven and keep onto the wire rack to cool in the pan for about 5 minutes.
10. Carefully, invert the muffins and serve warm.

GLENDALE
Grocery Rotisserie Dip

Prep Time: 10 mins
Total Time: 10 mins

Servings per Recipe: 30
Calories	154.7
Fat	11.6g
Cholesterol	31.0mg
Sodium	168.1mg
Carbohydrates	6.1g
Protein	6.9g

Ingredients

1 rotisserie-cooked chicken, shredded
1 red onion, diced
1 (12 oz.) cans green chilies
1 bunch cilantro, chopped
1 tomatoes, diced

1/2 C. Parmesan cheese, shredded
2 C. mayonnaise
2 C. sour cream
3 tbsp cumin

Directions

1. In a bowl, add all the ingredients and mix until well combined.
2. Serve immediately.

Barley
Bean Sprout Boxes

Prep Time: 10 mins
Total Time: 10 mins

Servings per Recipe: 2

Calories	492.0
Fat	28.1g
Cholesterol	31.0mg
Sodium	653.3mg
Carbohydrates	50.7g
Protein	15.4g

Ingredients

1 1/2 C. cooked barley
1 C. bean sprouts, any variety
1/3 C. crumbled Cotija cheese
1/4 C. sliced almonds, toasted
1/4 tsp kosher salt
1 small ripe avocado, peeled, pitted, and sliced
flaky salt
ground black pepper

Yogurt
1/2 C. plain yogurt
1 tsp grated lemon zest
1 tsp lemon juice
1 tbsp chopped fresh chives
1 pinch kosher salt

Directions

1. For the yogurt sauce: in a bowl, add all the ingredients and mi well.
2. In a small bowl, mix together the barley, almonds, sprouts, cheese and kosher salt.
3. Divide the barley mixture into 2 serving bowls and top with the avocado and yogurt sauce.
4. Serve with a sprinkling of the flaky salt and pepper.

CUPERTINO
Cashews Chickpeas

 Prep Time: 10 mins

Total Time: 40 mins

Servings per Recipe: 4

Calories	317.7
Fat	11.8g
Cholesterol	8.5mg
Sodium	394.8mg
Carbohydrates	44.2g
Protein	12.2g

Ingredients

1/2 C. raw cashews
1 C. non-dairy milk
1 garlic clove
1 large onion, sliced
2 carrots, chopped

1 (15 oz.) cans chickpeas
1 bunch kale, stems removed, leaves sliced
1/4 tsp crushed red pepper flakes

Directions

1. In a high speed blender, add the cashews, garlic and non-dairy milk and pulse until smooth.
2. In a large skillet, heat 2-3 tbsp of the water and sauté the onion and carrots for about 5 minutes.
3. Stir in the chickpeas and kale and sauté until kale starts to wilt, adding more water if needed.
4. Cook, covered for about 10 minutes.
5. Stir in the cashew sauce and red pepper and cook, uncovered for about 2-3 minutes.

California
Shrimp Bowls

🥣 Prep Time: 30 mins
🕐 Total Time: 45 mins

Servings per Recipe: 4
Calories	194.0
Fat	5.7g
Cholesterol	119.5mg
Sodium	716.1mg
Carbohydrates	19.8g
Protein	15.7g

Ingredients

1 1/3 C. cooked short-grain brown rice
2 tbsp rice vinegar
8 oz. cooked shrimp, peeled and tails removed
1 C. diced cucumber
1 tsp chopped fresh chives
1/2 C. mashed avocado

4 tsp sesame seeds
4 tsp reduced sodium soy sauce
4 tsp mayonnaise
1 tsp Sriracha sauce

Directions

1. Cook the rice according to package's directions, omitting oil and salt.
2. When rice is done, stir in the rice vinegar.
3. Spread rice onto a sheet pan to cool completely.
4. Cut shrimp into 1-inch cubes.
5. In a small bowl, mix together the cucumber and chives.
6. In another small bowl, mix together the mayonnaise and Sriracha sauce.
7. In a cup, place the layers about 1/4 C. of the cucumber, followed by 2 tbsp of avocado, 1/4 of the shrimp and 1/3 C. rice.
8. Carefully turn the cup upside down to turn the stack onto a plate, lightly tapping the bottom of the cup.
9. Repeat with the remaining ingredients.
10. Sprinkle each serving with Furikake and serve with a drizzling of the soy sauce and Sriracha mayonnaise.

3 CHEESE
Quesadilla

Prep Time: 15 mins
Total Time: 20 mins

Servings per Recipe: 3
Calories	420.7
Fat	29.9g
Cholesterol	23.1mg
Sodium	453.6mg
Carbohydrates	32.4g
Protein	10.7g

Ingredients

3 Hass avocadoes, halved and sliced
lime juice
olive oil
salt
1 1/2 C. manchego cheese, shredded
1 C. panela cheese, grated
1/2 C. Cotija cheese, shredded

ground black pepper
3 poblano chiles, roasted, peeled, strips
3 flour tortillas
unsalted butter
salsa fresca

Directions

1. Coat the avocado slices with lime juice and oil evenly and sprinkle with salt lightly.
2. Cook the avocado slices on grill until lightly browned with grill marks on both sides.
3. In a bowl, mix together all cheeses.
4. Place about 1/4 C. of the cheese mixture on half of each tortilla, followed by poblano strips, avocado slices, salsa and remaining cheese mixture.
5. Roll up the tortillas.
6. In a skillet, melt the butter over medium heat and cook the quesadillas until browned from both sides.
7. In the last minute of cooking, cover the pan.
8. Cut each quesadilla into 4 pieces and serve.

Pasadena
Polenta Salad

Prep Time: 30 mins
Total Time: 2 hrs 30 mins

Servings per Recipe: 4
Calories   398.3
Fat   27.1g
Cholesterol   0.0mg
Sodium   870.6mg
Carbohydrates   34.4g
Protein   8.5g

Ingredients

3 C. chicken broth
1 C. uncooked dry polenta
1/2 tsp salt
2 tsp onion powder
2 tsp ground coriander
1/2 tsp garlic powder
1/2 tsp ground birds eye peppers

2 reed avocados, peeled, pitted and cubed
1/3 C. chopped cilantro
3 tbsp olive oil

Directions

1. In a 2-quart pan, mix together the broth, ground coriander, onion powder, garlic powder, powdered chili and salt over medium-high heat and bring to a boil.
2. Add the polenta and stir to combine.
3. Reduce the heat to medium-low and cook for about 5 minutes, stirring continuously.
4. Remove from the heat and spread the polenta into a greased glass baking dish evenly.
5. Place a plastic wrap on the top of the polenta and press to remove any air bubbles.
6. Refrigerate for at least 2 hours.
7. With a knife, cut the polenta into cubes and transfer into a bowl.
8. Add the avocado, cilantro and oil and gently, stir to combine.
9. Serve at room temperature.

ANAHEIM
Corn Pizza

Prep Time: 10 mins
Total Time: 20 mins

Servings per Recipe: 4
Calories	166.5
Fat	11.6g
Cholesterol	33.3mg
Sodium	616.3mg
Carbohydrates	10.3g
Protein	6.9g

Ingredients

1 purchased baked 12-inch pizza crust
1 tbsp olive oil, plus
more olive oil, as needed
1/2 C. salsa
3/4 C. guacamole
1/2 C. corn kernel
1/2 C. thinly sliced green onion

1/4 C. chopped anaheim chili
1/4 C. chopped red bell pepper
1 C. feta cheese
1 tbsp chopped oregano

Directions

1. Set your oven to 450 degrees F before doing anything else.
2. Coat the pizza bread shell with the olive oil.
3. Place the salsa over shell, followed by the guacamole, vegetables, cheese and oregano.
4. Drizzle with 1 tbsp of the olive oil.
5. Cook in the oven for about 10 minutes.

Calabasas
Casserole

Prep Time: 5 mins

Total Time: 30 mins

Servings per Recipe: 4
Calories	442.7
Fat	31.8g
Cholesterol	86.7mg
Sodium	857.1mg
Carbohydrates	24.6g
Protein	18.3g

Ingredients

1 lb California-blend frozen vegetables (
broccoli, cauliflower, and carrots)
1 (14 3/4 oz.) cans creamed corn
1 C. sour cream
1/4 C. milk

2 C. cheddar cheese
1/4 tsp salt
1/2 tsp pepper

Directions

1. Set your oven to 350 degrees F before doing anything else.
2. In large bowl, add all the ingredients except 1 C. of the cheese.
3. Place the mixture into a 9X12-inch casserole dish and top with the remaining cheese.
4. Cook in the oven for about 20-25 minutes.

MONTEREY
Artichoke Quesadillas

 Prep Time: 25 mins

Total Time: 40 mins

Servings per Recipe: 6
Calories 445.7
Fat 25.5g
Cholesterol 57.1mg
Sodium 942.3mg
Carbohydrates 36.8g
Protein 18.1g

Ingredients

2 1/2 C. Monterey jack cheese, shredded
6 1/2 oz. marinated artichoke hearts, chopped
1/3 C. black olives, chopped
2/3 C. salsa

1/4 C. cilantro, chopped
12 soft taco-size flour tortillas
3 tbsp butter, melted

Directions

1. In a large bowl, mix together the cheese, olives, artichokes, salsa and cilantro.
2. Coat one side of 6 tortillas with the melted butter and place onto a baking sheet, butter side down.
3. Top each tortilla with the cheese mixture and cover with remaining tortillas and cot with the butter.
4. Cook in the oven for about 10 minutes.
5. Remove from the oven and keep aside to cool for about 5 minutes.
6. Cut into wedges and serve.

Mexican
Meringue Squares

🥣 Prep Time: 30 mins
🕐 Total Time: 1 hr

Servings per Recipe: 36
Calories	187.2
Fat	10.7g
Cholesterol	17.6mg
Sodium	104.3mg
Carbohydrates	21.3g
Protein	2.9g

Ingredients

1 C. shortening
1 1/2 C. packed brown sugar
1/2 C. sugar
3 eggs, separated
1 tbsp cold water
1 tbsp vanilla
2 C. all-purpose flour
1 tsp baking soda

1/8 tsp salt
1 C. semi-sweet chocolate chips
1 C. ground salted peanuts

Directions

1. Set your oven to 350 degrees F before doing anything else and lightly, grease a 15x10x1-inch baking dish.
2. In a bowl, add the shortening, 1/2 C brown sugar and 1/2 C sugar and beat until creamy.
3. Add the egg yolks and mix well.
4. In a small bowl, mix together the water and vanilla.
5. In another bowl, mix together the flour, baking soda and salt.
6. Add the flour mixture into the creamed mixture alternately with water mixture and mix well.
7. Place the mixture into prepared baking dish and sprinkle with the chocolate chips.
8. In a small glass bowl, add the egg whites and beat until soft peaks form.
9. Add the remaining brown sugar, 2 tbsp at a time, beating well after each addition until stiff peaks form.
10. Spread over egg white mixture over the chocolate chips and top with the peanuts.
11. Cook in the oven for about 30-35 minutes.

CALIFORNIA
Cucumbers with Dill Vinaigrette

 Prep Time: 10 mins
Total Time: 1 hr 10 mins

Servings per Recipe: 6
Calories	47.4
Fat	0.1g
Cholesterol	0.0mg
Sodium	102.3mg
Carbohydrates	10.0g
Protein	0.9g

Ingredients

3 cucumbers, sliced
1/4 C. snipped dill
1 C. cider vinegar
1/4 C. water
2 tbsp sugar

1/4 tsp salt
1 dash pepper
dill sprigs

Directions

1. In a large bowl, add the cucumber and dill.
2. In another bowl, add the vinegar, water, sugar, salt and pepper and mix until sugar is dissolved.
3. Pour vinegar mixture over cucumbers and toss to coat well.
4. Refrigerate, covered for at least 1 hour.
5. Serve with a garnishing of the dill sprigs.

Spicy Cheese & Walnut Log

Prep Time: 15 mins
Total Time: 1 hr 15 mins

Servings per Recipe: 1

Calories	1409.5
Fat	117.9g
Cholesterol	285.5mg
Sodium	2931.3mg
Carbohydrates	27.1g
Protein	66.7g

Ingredients

6 oz. cream cheese, softened
2-3 cloves garlic, chopped
1/4 tsp salt
1/8-1/4 tsp cayenne pepper
8 oz. grated Monterey jack cheese

8 oz. crumbled blue cheese
1/2 C. chopped walnuts
2/3 C. crushed rye crackers

Directions

1. In a large bowl, add the cream cheese, garlic, cayenne and salt and beat until smooth.
2. Add the Monterey Jack, blue cheeses and walnuts and beat vigorously until well combined.
3. Refrigerate for about 2 hours.
4. Spread the rye cracker crumbs on a large plate.
5. Divide the cheese mixture in half and then shape each half into a log.
6. Coat each log in the cracker crumbs, pressing gently so the crackers stick.
7. With 1 plastic wrap, cover each cheese log and chill until serving time.

BREAD
Mountain View

Prep Time: 10 mins
Total Time: 1 hr 10 mins

Servings per Recipe: 1
Calories	4068.5
Fat	187.6g
Cholesterol	262.7mg
Sodium	5201.2mg
Carbohydrates	532.5g
Protein	83.7g

Ingredients

3 C. flour, sifted
1 C. sugar
4 tsp baking powder
1 1/2 tsp salt
1 1/2 C. chopped walnuts, divided

1 large egg, beaten
1/4 C. shortening, softened
1 1/2 C. milk
1 tsp vanilla

Directions

1. Set your oven to 350 degrees F before doing anything else and grease a loaf pan.
2. In a bowl, mix together the flour, 1 1/4 C. of the walnuts, sugar, baking powder and salt.
3. Add the egg, milk, shortening and vanilla and mix until just combined.
4. Place the mixture into the prepared loaf pan evenly and sprinkle with the remaining walnuts.
5. Cook in the oven for about 60-70 minutes.
6. Remove from the oven and keep onto the wire rack to cool in the pan for about 5 minutes.
7. Carefully, invert the bread onto the wire rack to cool completely before slicing.

Rice
& Seaweed Salad

Prep Time: 15 mins
Total Time: 1 hr

Servings per Recipe: 6

Calories	487.2
Fat	10.1g
Cholesterol	7.5mg
Sodium	665.4mg
Carbohydrates	87.4g
Protein	10.6g

Ingredients

3 C. uncooked sushi sticky rice
3 C. water
2 tbsp sesame seed oil
4 tbsp unseasoned rice vinegar
1 tbsp sugar
2 tbsp Kikkoman soy sauce
2 tbsp wasabi powder
8 oz. imitation crab meat

1/2 seedless cucumber, peel and slice
1 avocado, cubes
1/4 C. Japanese pickled ginger
1 sheet nori, seaweed sheets strips

Directions

1. Wash the rice and rinse completely.
2. In a medium pan, add the rice and water over high heat and bring to a boil.
3. Reduce the heat to low and simmer, covered for about 35 - 45 minutes.
4. Remove from the heat and keep aside to cool before using.
5. For the dressing: in a bowl, add the sesame oil, rice vinegar, sugar, soy sauce and wasabi powder and mix until well combined.
6. In a large bowl, add the cooked sushi rice, crab meat, cucumber, avocado, ginger and dressing and mix until well combined.
7. Serve with a topping of the sea weeded strips.

ARTICHOKE
Pizza

Prep Time: 20 mins
Total Time: 30 mins

Servings per Recipe: 6
Calories   145.8
Fat   10.5g
Cholesterol   26.7mg
Sodium   301.7mg
Carbohydrates   6.1g
Protein   7.4g

Ingredients

1 (2 1/2 oz.) envelopes tuna
1 large prepared pizza crust
2 tbsp olive oil
1 garlic clove, minced
1 (6 oz.) jars marinated artichoke hearts
1/2 red bell pepper, sliced

1/2 red onion, sliced
1 C. feta cheese, crumbled
1/4 C. basil, chopped

Directions

1. Set your oven to 450 degrees F before doing anything else.
2. Arrange the pizza crust onto a baking sheet.
3. In a small skillet, heat the olive oil over medium heat and sauté the garlic for about 30 seconds.
4. Spread the garlic oil over the pizza crust evenly and top with the flaked tuna, followed by the red peppers, artichokes, red onion, feta cheese and basil.
5. Cook in the oven for about 8-10 minutes.

California
Mesa Fries

🥣 Prep Time: 15 mins
🕐 Total Time: 35 mins

Servings per Recipe: 1
Calories   515.4
Fat   28.7g
Cholesterol   56.7mg
Sodium   1323.2mg
Carbohydrates   45.7g
Protein   20.3g

Ingredients

1/2 tsp ground cayenne pepper
2 tsp mesquite powder
1/2 tsp celery salt
1 tsp garlic powder
spray olive oil
24 oz. frozen French fries
1 C. California Monterey jack cheese, shredded

3/4 C. bottled chunky blue cheese
1/2 C. California blue cheese, crumbled
2 stalks celery, trimmed and minced
4 green onions, sliced

Directions

1. Set your oven to 450 degrees F before doing anything else.
2. In a bowl, mix together the mesquite seasoning, cayenne, celery salt and garlic powder. Keep aside.
3. Spray the frozen fries with the olive oil evenly and sprinkle with the seasonings.
4. Arrange the fried onto a baking sheet in a single layer and cook in the oven according to manufacturer's directions, flipping once in the middle way.
5. Remove from the oven and top with shredded Monterey Jack cheese.
6. Cook in the oven for about 30 seconds.
7. Remove from the oven and immediately, drizzle with the blue cheese dressing, followed by crumbled Blue cheese, celery and green onion.
8. Serve immediately.

FULL
Oatmeal Cookies

🥣 Prep Time: 20 mins
🕐 Total Time: 35 mins

Servings per Recipe: 1	
Calories	1782.4
Fat	71.0g
Cholesterol	99.4mg
Sodium	1154.5mg
Carbohydrates	266.0g
Protein	33.8g

Ingredients

1 C. butter, softened
2 1/4 C. brown sugar, packed
1 tbsp maple flavoring
1/2 tsp vanilla extract
1 (14 oz.) cans crushed pineapple in juice
3 1/3 C. all-purpose flour
3/4 C. skim milk powder
2 tsp baking soda

2 tsp cinnamon
1/2 tsp salt
3 1/3 C. quick-cooking oatmeal
1 C. raisins
1 C. chopped dates
2 C. California walnuts, chopped

Directions

1. Set your oven to 350 degrees F before doing anything else and grease a large cookie sheet.
2. In large bowl, add the sugar and butter and with an electric mixer, beat until fluffy.
3. Add the maple flavoring and vanilla and mi well.
4. Stir in the pineapple and juice.
5. In another bowl, mix together the flour, baking soda, milk powder, cinnamon and salt.
6. Add the flour mixture into the pineapple mixture and mix until just combined. Fold in the oatmeal, raisins and walnuts.
7. With a rounded spoonful, drop the mixture onto the prepared cookie sheet in a single layer.
8. Cook in the oven for about 12-15 minutes.
9. Remove from the oven and keep onto the wire rack to cool in the pan for about 5 minutes.
10. Carefully, invert the cookies onto the wire rack to cool completely.

Fruity

Mushroom Salad with Garlic Vinaigrette

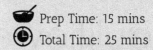 Prep Time: 15 mins

Total Time: 25 mins

Servings per Recipe: 6

Calories	299.4
Fat	25.3g
Cholesterol	2.7mg
Sodium	184.1mg
Carbohydrates	18.4g
Protein	4.3g

Ingredients

Mushroom Salad
1 (10 oz.) packet ready-to-eat spinach
2-3 large ripe pears, quartered and sliced
1 California avocado, peeled and diced
3-4 slices turkey bacon, cooked crisp and crumbled
1/2 C. pine nuts, toasted
1/2 C. dried cranberries

1/4 C. sliced mushrooms
Vinaigrette
1/3 C. olive oil
2 tbsp seasoned rice vinegar
1 garlic clove, crushed
1/4 tsp salt
1-2 tsp Dijon mustard

Directions

1. For the salad: in a serving bowl, mix together all ingredients.
2. In a small bowl, add all the dressing ingredients and beat until well combined.
3. Pour dressing over salad and toss to coat well.
4. Serve immediately.

SANTA CLARA
Cauliflower

Prep Time: 5 mins
Total Time: 45 mins

Servings per Recipe: 4
Calories   142.9
Fat   7.8g
Cholesterol   33.0mg
Sodium   364.8mg
Carbohydrates   12.5g
Protein   7.7g

Ingredients

1 head cauliflower, chopped
1/2 C. sun dried tomato and oregano
salad dressing

1/2-1 C. cheddar cheese

Directions

1. Set your oven to 350 degrees F before doing anything else.
2. In a steamer, steam the cauliflower for about 5 minutes.
3. In a medium casserole dish, add the cauliflower and salad dressing and toss to coat.
4. Cook in the oven for about 30 minutes.
5. Sprinkle with the cheese and cook in the oven for about 5 minutes more.

Santa Monica
Ice Cream

Prep Time: 20 mins
Total Time: 20 mins

Servings per Recipe: 8
Calories	282.9
Fat	16.9g
Cholesterol	53.6mg
Sodium	117.8mg
Carbohydrates	30.2g
Protein	4.0g

Ingredients

6-8 large ripe kiwi fruits
3/4 C. sugar
1 (8 oz.) packet cream cheese, softened
2 C. half-and-half milk

2 tsp vanilla extract
pureed kiwi and crumbled graham cracker crust

Directions

1. Cut kiwi in half and scoop out the flesh.
2. In a small food processor, add kiwi flesh and pulse until pureed.
3. In a medium pan, add kiwi puree over medium-low heat for about 15-20 minutes, stirring frequently.
4. Remove from heat and keep aside to cool.
5. In a bowl, add the cream cheese and sugar and beat until smooth.
6. Slowly, add half-and-half, beating continuously until well combined.
7. Stir in the kiwi puree and vanilla.
8. Refrigerate to chill completely.
9. Transfer the mixture into an ice cream maker and process according to manufacturer's instructions.
10. Not, transfer into an airtight container and freeze before serving.
11. Serve with a topping of the crumbled graham cracker crust.

MEXI-CALI
Harissa

Prep Time: 40 mins
Total Time: 48 mins

Servings per Recipe: 1
Calories	301.7
Fat	24.2g
Cholesterol	0.0mg
Sodium	2921.8mg
Carbohydrates	20.9g
Protein	4.6g

Ingredients

4 oz. dried guajillo chilies
2 tsp caraway seeds
2 tsp coriander seeds
1 tsp cumin seed
1 tsp dried mint

1 1/2 tsp salt
2 tbsp olive oil
1 Mexican lime

Directions

1. Remove the stems and the seeds from the chilies.
2. In a non-stick frying pan, add the chilies over very high heat and roast for couple minutes.
3. Transfer the chilies in a large bowl of boiling water for at least 40 minutes.
4. In the same frying pan, roast the caraway, coriander and cumin seeds until the seeds begin to pop.
5. Transfer the seeds into a spice mill with the mint and grind into a powder.
6. Drain the chilies and chop them roughly.
7. In a food processor, add the chilies, garlic, oil, lemon juice, spices and salt and pulse until a smooth paste is formed.
8. Transfer the harissa in a glass jar and cover with oil.
9. Preserve for up to 12 weeks.

Baja
Breakfast (Glazed Benedict Eggs)

🥣 Prep Time: 10 mins
🕐 Total Time: 20 mins

Servings per Recipe: 4
Calories	432.1
Fat	35.2g
Cholesterol	325.3mg
Sodium	362.0mg
Carbohydrates	18.2g
Protein	12.4g

Ingredients

2 English muffins
4 slices turkey bacon
1 avocado
salt
pepper
butter
4 eggs
snipped fresh cilantro, to garnish

Mesa Glaze
1/4 C. butter
2 egg yolks
1/4 C. heavy cream
1 tbsp lemon juice
1/2 tsp Dijon mustard
1-2 tbsp minced chipotle chile in adobo

Directions

1. For the Hollandaise sauce: cut the butter into 2 pieces.
2. In a glass bowl, add the butter and cover with a paper towel.
3. Microwave on High for about 30-45 seconds.
4. Remove butter from the microwave and stir until completely melted.
5. In a small bowl, add the egg yolks and with a whisk, beat well.
6. Add beaten egg yolks into the butter and stir well.
7. Add the cream and lemon juice and stir to combine well.
8. Microwave, uncovered on High for about 1-1 1/2 minutes, stirring after every 20 seconds.
9. Remove sauce from microwave and stir in mustard and minced chipotle.
10. Split English muffins in half and toast until browned.
11. Heat a skillet and cook the bacon until crisp.
12. Cut the avocado in half and remove the pit.
13. Scoop flesh into a bowl and with a pinch of salt and pepper and with a fork, mash completely.

14. In a small pan, melt 1-2 tsp of the butter over medium-low heat.
15. Break two eggs into pan and reduce heat to low.
16. Cook eggs over until whites are done, and yolks are still runny).
17. Repeat with remaining two eggs.
18. Spread the mashed avocado over the toasted English muffin halves and top with the bacon.
19. Place eggs on top of the bacon, then drizzle each with mesa glaze.
20. Serve with a sprinkling of the cilantro.

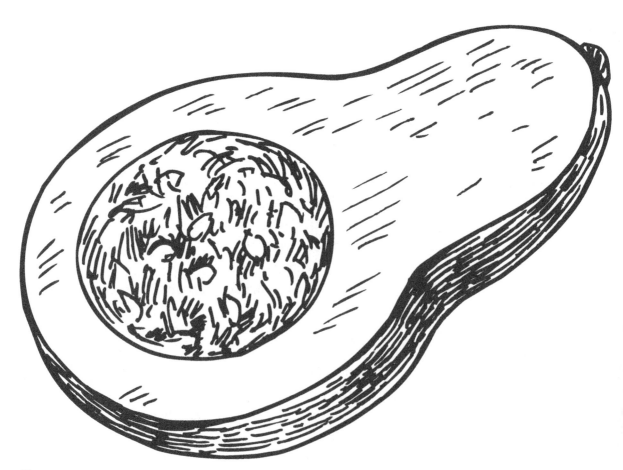

Avocado
Chapati

Prep Time: 15 mins
Total Time: 15 mins

Servings per Recipe: 4

Calories	529.2
Fat	33.2g
Cholesterol	63.8mg
Sodium	637.9mg
Carbohydrates	47.6g
Protein	12.8g

Ingredients

4 chapattis
1 C. cream cheese, softened
1 ripe avocado, peeled, pitted and sliced
8 lettuce leaves

2 medium tomatoes, sliced
1 small sweet onion, sliced in rings
1 C. alfalfa, spouts

Directions

1. Arrange the chapattis onto a smooth surface.
2. Spread cream cheese down the center of each chapatti evenly and top with avocado slices, followed by lettuce, tomato slices, onion rings and sprouts.
3. Serve immediately.

FRESNO
Pilaf

Prep Time: 30 mins
Total Time: 1 hr 30 mins

Servings per Recipe: 6
Calories   291.3
Fat   15.6g
Cholesterol   51.4mg
Sodium   1006.9mg
Carbohydrates   21.2g
Protein   16.7g

Ingredients

3/4 C. ripe olives
1 lb. ground beef
1 tbsp salad oil
1/3 C. green pepper, chopped
2/3 C. onion, chopped
1/2 C. white rice, uncooked
1 1/2 tsp salt

1/4 tsp pepper
2 C. hot water
1 (6 oz.) cans tomato paste

Directions

1. Set your oven to 350 degrees F before doing anything else and lightly, grease a casserole dish.
2. Cut olives into wedges.
3. In a skillet, heat the oil and cook the ground beef until browned completely.
4. With a plotted spoon, transfer the beef into a prepared casserole dish, reserving the grease.
5. In the same skillet, add the onion and bell pepper and sauté until tender.
6. Transfer the onion mixture into casserole dish with beef.
7. In the same skillet, add the rice and toast lightly, stirring continuously.
8. Transfer the rice into casserole dish with beef.
9. Add olives and stir to combine.
10. In a bowl, mix together the tomato paste and hot water.
11. Pour tomato paste mixture over rice mixture evenly.
12. Cook in the oven for about 1 hour.

Baja
Avocado Salad

Prep Time: 20 mins
Total Time: 20 mins

Servings per Recipe: 6
Calories	434.6
Fat	37.4g
Cholesterol	35.6mg
Sodium	626.4mg
Carbohydrates	23.1 g
Protein	9.5g

Ingredients

3 large avocados, diced
2 large lemons, juiced
2 large tomatoes, chopped
2 C. jicama, peeled & diced

8 oz. feta cheese, crumbled
4 oz. black olives, pitted & sliced
4 tbsp olive oil

Directions

1. Place the avocado slices onto a serving platter in a single layer and drizzle with 1/3 of the lemon juice.
2. Place the tomatoes on top of the avocados, followed by the jicama and drizzle with half of the remaining lemon juice.
3. Now, place the rumbled cheese on top, followed by the olives and drizzle with the remaining lemon juice and olive oil.
4. Refrigerate for about 4-6 hours before serving.

NORTHERN
Onion Dip

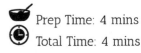

Prep Time: 4 mins
Total Time: 4 mins

Servings per Recipe: 4
Calories	127.1
Fat	5.2g
Cholesterol	17.1mg
Sodium	556.8mg
Carbohydrates	4.5g
Protein	14.9g

Ingredients

1/4 C. skim milk
2 C. creamed small curd cottage cheese
1 1/2 oz. dry onion soup

Directions

1. In a blender, add the cottage cheese and skim milk and pulse on high speed until smooth.
2. Transfer into a bowl and stir in onion soup mix.
3. Refrigerate, covered at least 1 hour.

Chihuahua
Sausage Soup

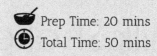
 Prep Time: 20 mins
 Total Time: 50 mins

Servings per Recipe: 6
Calories   688.0
Fat   55.4g
Cholesterol   138.4mg
Sodium   704.9mg
Carbohydrates   20.0g
Protein   33.5g

Ingredients

2 tbsp vegetable oil
1 large onion, sliced
20 garlic cloves, chopped
1 red bell pepper, seeded, and sliced
1/4 tsp ground cumin
6 C. low sodium chicken broth
2 (14 oz.) cans unsweetened coconut milk
2 chipotle peppers, minced
1 (15 oz.) cans red pinto beans, drained
8 oz. boneless skinless chicken thighs strips

8 oz. Mexican beef sausage
8 oz. shrimp, peeled, deveined, and chopped
2 tbsp lime juice
1 few dashes hot sauce
salt
fresh ground black pepper
2/3 C. sweetened flaked coconut, toasted
1/2 C. cilantro leaves, chopped
avocado, slices
lime slice

Directions

1. In a large pan, heat 1 tbsp of the oil over medium heat and cook the onion for about 4 minutes, stirring occasionally.
2. Add red peppers, 10 cloves garlic and cumin and cook for about 2 minutes.
3. Add the chicken stock, coconut milk, chipotle peppers and 1 tbsp of the adobo sauce and bring to a boil. Reduce the heat to low and stir in pinto beans.
4. Meanwhile, in a large skillet, heat 1 tbsp of the oil over medium-high heat and cook the chicken for about 3 minutes.
5. Add sausage and 6 cloves garlic and cook for about 3 minutes.
6. Transfer the chicken mixture, shrimp, lime juice, and hot sauce into the simmering soup and cook for about 3-4 minutes.
7. Stir in the remaining 4 cloves garlic, salt and pepper and remove from the heat.
8. Serve immediately with the topping of the shredded coconut, cilantro, avocado slices and lime slices.

MEDJOOL
Milk Shake

Prep Time: 5 mins
Total Time: 5 mins

Servings per Recipe: 1
Calories	494.4
Fat	22.1g
Cholesterol	87.7mg
Sodium	174.5mg
Carbohydrates	70.2g
Protein	9.1g

Ingredients

4 pitted dates, chopped
1/4 C. very cold milk
1 1/4 C. high-quality vanilla ice cream

Directions

1. In a high speed blender, add all the ingredients and pulse until frothy.
2. Serve immediately.

Herbed
Sonoma Oil

Prep Time: 10 mins
Total Time: 10 mins

Servings per Recipe: 1

Calories	245.5
Fat	27.0g
Cholesterol	0.0mg
Sodium	1.6mg
Carbohydrates	1.5g
Protein	0.3g

Ingredients

1/4 C. extra virgin olive oil
2 cloves garlic
1/4 tsp dried oregano
1/4 tsp dried basil
1/2 tsp dried parsley

1/4 tsp dried marjoram
1/4 tsp red pepper flakes
1/4 tsp ground black pepper

Directions

1. In a blender, add all the ingredients and pulse until pureed.
2. Store in a small covered jar.

HOW TO
Make Chitlins

Prep Time: 1 hr 30 mins
Total Time: 6 hrs 30 mins

Servings per Recipe: 6
Calories	1427.7
Fat	125.9 g
Cholesterol	1166.2 mg
Sodium	2526.7 mg
Carbohydrates	10.1 g
Protein	59.2 g

Ingredients

10 lb. chitterlings
1 C. onion, diced
1 C. celery, diced
6 small hot pepper
3 garlic cloves, minced
2 tbsp salt
1 tbsp black pepper

1 C. cider vinegar
1 tbsp sugar

Directions

1. In a bowl of the salted warm water, soak the chitterlings for about 30 minutes.
2. Cut each into 12-inch pieces and remove all fat particles and debris.
3. Wash in warm to hot water 3-5 times.
4. In a large Dutch oven, place the chitterlings pieces, onion, celery, peppers, garlic, salt and pepper and bring to a boil.
5. Reduce the heat to medium-low and simmer for about 4 hours.
6. Add vinegar and sugar and stir to combine.
7. Reduce the heat to low and simmer for about 1 hour.

Turkey Burgers
with Fruit Salsa

🥣 Prep Time: 15 mins
🕐 Total Time: 30 mins

Servings per Recipe: 1
Calories	177.4
Fat	6.0g
Cholesterol	37.8mg
Sodium	337.9mg
Carbohydrates	19.9g
Protein	11.0g

Ingredients

2 1/2 C. figs, diced
1/2 C. red bell pepper, diced
1/2 C. golden raisin
2 green onions, sliced
1 jalapeño pepper, stemmed, seeded and minced
1 tbsp lemon juice
1/2 tsp ground ginger
20 oz. lean ground turkey

1 C. fig, minced dried
1/4 C. green onion, sliced
2 tbsp herbs, chopped, such as marjoram, thyme, rosemary and sage
3/4 tsp sea salt
1 C. arugula, baby leaves
12 dinner rolls, small, cut in half

Directions

1. For the salsa: in a bowl, add all the ingredients and mix.
2. Refrigerate, covered to chill before serving.
3. Set your grill for medium-high heat and generously, grease the grill grate.
4. For sliders: in a bowl, add the turkey, figs, green onions, herbs and salt and mix until well combined.
5. Make 12 small, flat burgers from the mixture.
6. Cook the burgers on the grill for about 3-5 minutes per side.
7. Arrange a few arugula leaves on bottom half of each roll and top with turkey burger and salsa.
8. Cover with the tops.
9. Serve alongside remaining salsa.

FIGS
with Mascarpone

Prep Time: 10 mins
Total Time: 11 mins

Servings per Recipe: 24	
Calories	45.2
Fat	0.1g
Cholesterol	0.0mg
Sodium	0.5mg
Carbohydrates	11.7g
Protein	0.4g

Ingredients

1 C. mascarpone cheese
1 tbsp crystallized ginger, chopped
2 1/2 tbsp sugar
1/8 tsp vanilla
26 fresh figs, ripe yet firm

mint sprig
cracker, sweet round

Directions

1. In a bowl, add the mascarpone, sugar, crystallized ginger and vanilla and mi until well combined.
2. Refrigerate, covered to chill.
3. For a fig platter: place the mascarpone mixture onto cold plate.
4. Arrange the figs around the mascarpone mixture and serve with a garnishing of the mint sprigs alongside the sweet crackers.

California
Pot Pie

Prep Time: 10 mins
Total Time: 50 mins

Servings per Recipe: 1
Calories	1965.5
Fat	80.8g
Cholesterol	475.9mg
Sodium	5693.1mg
Carbohydrates	170.1g
Protein	133.1g

Ingredients

1 (16 oz.) packet vegetables
2 C. cooked chicken, chopped
1 (10 oz.) cans cream of potato soup
1 C. low-fat milk
1 C. cheddar cheese, grated

1 white onion, fried
1/2 tsp salt
2 garlic cloves, diced
1 (8 oz.) packaged crescent roll dough

Directions

1. Set your oven to 375 degrees F before doing anything else and lightly, grease a 13x9x2-inch baking dish.
2. In a large bowl, mix together the chicken, vegetables, onions, soup, milk, cheese and salt.
3. Transfer the mixture into the prepared baking dish.
4. Unroll the crescent roll dough and separate into two rectangles.
5. Cut the dough into 1/2-inch strips.
6. Arrange the dough strips over the chicken mixture into a lattice pattern.
7. Cook in the oven for about 35-40 minutes.

PISTACHIO
Glazed Chicken

Prep Time: 15 mins
Total Time: 35 mins

Servings per Recipe: 4
Calories	154.4
Fat	7.6g
Cholesterol	34.2mg
Sodium	40.1mg
Carbohydrates	6.0g
Protein	15.5g

Ingredients

2 whole boneless skinless chicken
breasts, halved
1/4 tsp ground black pepper
1 tbsp oil
1/2 C. orange juice

2 tbsp water
2 tsp balsamic vinegar
2 green onions, sliced
1/4 C. chopped pistachios

Directions

1. With a meat mallet, pound chicken breasts to 1/2-inch thickness and season with pepper.
2. In a skillet, heat the oil and sear the chicken for about 2-3 minutes per side.
3. In the skillet, add the orange juice, water and balsamic vinegar and simmer covered for 10 minutes.
4. Transfer the chicken to a platter and keep warm.
5. In the sauce, add green onions and pistachios over medium heat until slightly thickened.
6. Place the sauce over chicken and serve.

Authentic
Street Pico De Gallo

🥣 Prep Time: 20 mins
🕐 Total Time: 20 mins

Servings per Recipe: 100
Calories	3.3
Fat	0.0g
Cholesterol	0.0mg
Sodium	7.1mg
Carbohydrates	0.7g
Protein	0.1g

Ingredients

5-6 large tomatoes, chopped
1-2 green chili pepper, chopped
3-4 jalapeños, chopped
Tabasco sauce
cayenne pepper
1-2 bushel cilantro, chopped
Worcestershire sauce, to taste

1 chopped med white onion
1 chopped med yellow onion
2 chopped green onions
1-2 C. tomato juice
1-2 tsp salt and pepper

Directions

1. In a bowl, add all the ingredients and mi well.
2. Transfer into a large jar and store into the refrigerator.

COUSCOUS
with Grapes

Prep Time: 10 mins
Total Time: 10 mins

Servings per Recipe: 4
Calories	250.8
Fat	3.8g
Cholesterol	0.0mg
Sodium	294.2mg
Carbohydrates	46.3g
Protein	8.5g

Ingredients

1 1/2 C. chicken broth
1/4 tsp ground black pepper
1 C. uncooked couscous
2 tbsp lemon juice
1 1/2 C. California seedless grapes

1/4 C. chopped fresh parsley
1 tbsp chopped green onion
2 tbsp pine nuts

Directions

1. In a small pan, add the broth and pepper and bring to a boil.
2. Add the couscous and lemon juice and mix well.
3. Cover the pan and remove from heat.
4. Keep aside, covered for about 5 minute.
5. Add the remaining ingredients and gently, toss to coat.

California
Mixed Vegetable Skillet

Prep Time: 5 mins
Total Time: 30 mins

Servings per Recipe: 4
Calories	233.9
Fat	2.2g
Cholesterol	65.8mg
Sodium	154.1mg
Carbohydrates	22.9g
Protein	31.8g

Ingredients

4 (1/4 lb.) boneless skinless chicken breast half
3 C. frozen mixed vegetables, thawed, drained
1/4 C. pesto sauce
1/4 C. water
1/2 C. shredded mozzarella cheese

Directions

1. Heat large greased skillet over medium-high heat.
2. Add chicken and cook, covered for about 5 minute per side.
3. Add the vegetables, pesto and water and bring to a boil.
4. Reduce the heat to medium and cook for about 6-8 minute, stirring occasionally.
5. Sprinkle with the cheese and immediately, cover the skillet.
6. Remove from heat and keep aside for about 5 minute before serving.

LINGUINE
Salad

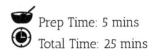 Prep Time: 5 mins
Total Time: 25 mins

Servings per Recipe: 4
Calories   476.1
Fat   26.9g
Cholesterol   21.5mg
Sodium   478.6mg
Carbohydrates   38.0g
Protein   21.2g

Ingredients

1 (6 1/2 oz.) cans solid tuna packed in
water, drained
1/2 C. frozen peas, thawed
1/2 C. roasted red pepper, strips
1/3 C. olive oil
1/3 C. blanched almond, toasted
1 tbsp chopped dill

1 tbsp lemon juice
6 oz. linguine
2 tbsp chopped parsley
2 tbsp Parmesan cheese, grated

Directions

1. In a large bowl, mix together the tuna, peas, roasted red pepper, olive oil, almonds, dill and
    lemon juice.
2. In a pan of salted boiling water, cook the pasta according to package's directions.
3. Drain the pasta ell.
4. Add the pasta and parsley into the bowl with tuna mixture and toss to coat.
5. Serve with a sprinkling of the Parmesan cheese.

California
Coconut Bars

🥣 Prep Time: 15 mins
🕐 Total Time: 35 mins

Servings per Recipe: 1
Calories	207.8
Fat	9.4g
Cholesterol	41.3mg
Sodium	270.0mg
Carbohydrates	29.3g
Protein	2.6g

Ingredients

1 C. granulated sugar
1 C. all-purpose flour
1 tsp salt
1 tbsp baking powder
2 large eggs
1/2 C. heated milk
1 tsp butter

1 tsp vanilla
1 C. coconut
6 tbsp evaporated milk
6 tbsp butter
10 tbsp brown sugar

Directions

1. Set your oven to 375 degrees F before doing anything else and grease an 8-inch cake pan.
2. In a large bowl, sift together the flour, sugar, baking powder and salt.
3. Add the eggs, butter, warmed milk and vanilla and beat until well combined.
4. Place the mixture into the prepared cake pan.
5. Cook in the oven for about 20 minutes.
6. Meanwhile, for topping: in a bowl, add the coconut, evaporated milk, butter, and brown sugar and mix until thick.
7. Remove the pan from the oven and spread the coconut mixture on base evenly.
8. Cook in the oven until brown and bubbly.
9. Remove from the oven and keep onto a wire rack cool completely before serving.
10. Cut into bars and serve.

GRAPEFRUIT
& Avocado Lunch Box Salad

Prep Time: 20 mins
Total Time: 20 mins

Servings per Recipe: 2
Calories	351.5
Fat	28.4g
Cholesterol	0.0mg
Sodium	8.7mg
Carbohydrates	26.5g
Protein	3.1g

Ingredients

1 pink grapefruit
1 avocado, halved
2 tbsp extra virgin olive oil
3 tbsp grapefruit juice
1 tsp brown sugar
1 tbsp minced red onion
2 tsp coriander leaves, chopped

salt & pepper
2 C. mixed baby greens

Directions

1. With a small sharp knife, cut off peel and white pith from the grapefruit.
2. Cut grapefruit into 4 slices crosswise.
3. In a small bowl, add the grapefruit juice, olive oil, sugar, onion, coriander, salt and pepper and beat until well combined.
4. Ina bowl, add the greens and 2 tbsp of the dressing and toss to coat well.
5. Divide greens onto 2 serving plates and top with grapefruit slices and avocado.
6. Drizzle with the remaining dressing and serve.

Silicone
Shrimp Appetizer

Prep Time: 10 mins
Total Time: 10 mins

Servings per Recipe: 8
Calories	171.1
Fat	5.4g
Cholesterol	159.4mg
Sodium	269.4mg
Carbohydrates	6.7g
Protein	22.8g

Ingredients

2 oz. sharp cheddar cheese
avocado, sliced
16 Triscuit crackers
8 small cooked clean shrimp, cut in half

2 tbsp thick chunky salsa

Directions

1. Cut cheese into 8 slices and then, each slice in half diagonally.
2. Cut avocado slices in half crosswise.
3. Top crackers with cheese, followed by avocados, shrimp and salsa.
4. Serve immediately.

AVOCADO
& Gorgonzola Salad

 Prep Time: 30 mins

Total Time: 40 mins

Servings per Recipe: 2

Calories	488.4
Fat	37.6g
Cholesterol	6.3mg
Sodium	272.2mg
Carbohydrates	37.8g
Protein	7.5g

Ingredients

1/4 C. honey
1/4 C. extra virgin olive oil
2 tbsp lemon juice
2 tsp vinegar
1/4 tsp salt
1/2 tsp celery seed
1/2 tsp ground mustard
1/2 tsp paprika
1/4 tsp onion powder
4 C. mixed salad greens

2 avocados, sliced
2 oranges, peeled and sectioned
1/2 C. slivered almonds, toasted
1/4 C. Gorgonzola, crumbled
1 small red onion, sliced

Directions

1. In a small bowl, add the honey, oil, lemon juice, vinegar, salt, celery seed, mustard, paprika and onion powder and beat until well combined.
2. In serving bowl, place the salad greens, avocados and orange pieces.
3. Pour the dressing and gently toss to coat well.
4. Serve with a topping of the almonds, cheese and onion.

Calamari
California

🍲 Prep Time: 10 mins
🕐 Total Time: 20 mins

Servings per Recipe: 4
Calories   457.2
Fat   21.4g
Cholesterol   103.5mg
Sodium   1053.3mg
Carbohydrates   42.5g
Protein   23.2g

Ingredients

4 calamari fillets
1/2 lb. Monterey jack cheese
4 oz. mild green chilies
4 oz. sweet red peppers

1 egg, beaten
2 C. breadcrumbs
oil

Directions

1. Arrange Monterey Jack cheese strips, green chilies and red chilies in the center of each Grande Calamari fillet.
2. Roll steak into a tube shape and secure with toothpicks.
3. Dip each roll into egg and then coat with breadcrumbs.
4. In a deep skillet, heat the oil to 350 degrees F and deep fry the rolls for about 4 minutes.
5. Transfer onto with paper towels-lined plate to drain.
6. Serve hot.

MEATBALLS
Stew

Prep Time: 15 mins
Total Time: 1 hr

Servings per Recipe: 4

Calories	477.1
Fat	25.3g
Cholesterol	101.2mg
Sodium	288.5mg
Carbohydrates	36.0g
Protein	25.5g

Ingredients

1 lb. ground meat
1 onion, peeled and minced
1 C. tomatoes
2 green bell peppers, seeded and chopped
1 quart water
1 potato, peeled and diced

salt
4 slices toast

Directions

1. Make marble-sized balls from the ground meat.
2. In a skillet, add the peppers, onion, tomatoes and water and bring to a boil.
3. Carefully, stir in the meatballs and simmer for about 30 minutes.
4. Add potatoes and salt and cook for about 10 minutes.
5. Serve stew alongside toast.

Blackberry
& Orange Pie

Prep Time: 20 mins
Total Time: 55 mins

Servings per Recipe: 6
Calories   478.4
Fat   20.5g
Cholesterol   0.0mg
Sodium   330.0mg
Carbohydrates   70.1g
Protein   6.0g

Ingredients

5 C. blackberries
1/2 C. sugar
1/4 C. water
1/4 C. orange marmalade
3 tbsp cornstarch
4 drops blackberry flavoring
2 (9 inch) pie crusts, unbaked but frozen

1 egg white, beaten
1 tbsp sugar

Directions

1. Set your oven to 375 degrees F before doing anything else and arrange a rack in the center of oven.
2. In a medium pan, add the sugar, marmalade and 1/4 C. of the water over medium heat and bring to a boil.
3. Remove from the heat and stir in half of the berries.
4. Add the cornstarch mixture and stir until well combined.
5. Return to heat and cook until thickened, stirring continuously.
6. Stir in the remaining berries and the blackberry flavoring and remove from the heat.
7. Place the hot berry mixture into the frozen pie shell.
8. Cut the pieces from another pie shell for the top.
9. Arrange the pieces over the top of the pie, leaving spaces in between for venting.
10. Coat the top with egg white and sprinkle with sugar.
11. Cook in the oven for about 35 minutes.
12. Remove from the oven and keep aside to cool before serving.

MARIA'S
Pico De Gallo

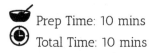
Servings per Recipe: 8
Calories   17.9
Fat   0.1g
Cholesterol   0.0mg
Sodium   4.1mg
Carbohydrates   3.9g
Protein   0.6g

Ingredients

2 C. tomatoes, diced
1 C. yellow onion, diced
1 C. cilantro, chopped

1 tsp celery seed

Directions

1. In a bowl, add all the ingredients and mix well.
2. Serve immediately.

California
Burgers

🥣 Prep Time: 10 mins
🕐 Total Time: 1 hr 10 mins

Servings per Recipe: 4
Calories   624.6
Fat   36.2g
Cholesterol   122.4mg
Sodium   674.5mg
Carbohydrates   40.2g
Protein   33.4g

Ingredients

3 tbsp unsalted butter
2 C. yellow onions, sliced
1 lb. ground beef
2 tsp Worcestershire sauce
salt and pepper

8 slices rye bread
4 oz. goat cheese
mustard, your choice

Directions

1. In a medium skillet, melt the butter over medium heat and stir in the onion.
2. Reduce the heat to low and cook, covered for about 15 minutes, stirring occasionally.
3. Uncover and cook for about 45 minutes, stirring frequently.
4. Set the broiler of your oven and grease a broiler pan.
5. In a large bowl, mix together the ground beef, Worcestershire sauce, salt and pepper.
6. Make 8 equal sized patties from the mixture.
7. Cut the cheese into 4 pieces a little smaller that the patties.
8. Place a piece of cheese on 4 of the patties, cover with the remaining patties, and press edges together to seal.
9. Arrange the patties onto prepared broiler pan.
10. Cook under the broiler for about 4 minutes per side.
11. During the last few minutes of cooking, place the bread slices on the outer edges of the broiler pan to toast.
12. Top 4 slices of the bread with the patties and caramelized onion.
13. Cover with the remaining bread slices and serve.

HOW TO
Make Shortbread

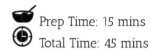

Prep Time: 15 mins
Total Time: 45 mins

Servings per Recipe: 24	
Calories	97.4
Fat	7.1g
Cholesterol	11.2mg
Sodium	69.0mg
Carbohydrates	7.2g
Protein	1.6g

Ingredients

3/4 C. flour
1/2 C. cornstarch
1/4 C. icing sugar
1/2 tsp salt
1/2 C. ground walnut
1/2 C. unsalted butter, softened

1/4 C. blue cheese
1/2 tsp grated lemon zest
24 walnut halves

Directions

1. Set your oven to 275 degrees F before doing anything else and line a baking sheet with the parchment paper.
2. In a bowl, mix together the flour, cornstarch, icing sugar, ground walnuts and salt.
3. Add butter, blue cheese and lemon zest and with your hands, knead until a soft dough ball is formed.
4. Using a small scoop, shape the dough into half-spheres and then press a walnut half into the top of each cookie.
5. Arrange cookies onto prepared baking sheet.
6. Cook in the oven for about 27-30 minutes.
7. Remove from the oven and keep onto the wire rack to cool in the pan for about 5 minutes.
8. Carefully, invert the cookies onto the wire rack to cool completely.

Deep
Fudge Cake

Prep Time: 20 mins
Total Time: 1 hr 40 mins

Servings per Recipe: 24
Calories	392.7
Fat	19.4g
Cholesterol	69.5mg
Sodium	135.4mg
Carbohydrates	54.2g
Protein	6.1g

Ingredients

3/4 C. butter
2 1/2 C. sugar
6 eggs
6 oz. unsweetened chocolate, melted
1 1/2 tsp vanilla
1 C. milk
3 C. flour
1 tbsp baking powder

1/4 tsp salt
3 C. dates, chopped and tossed
1 1/2 tbsp flour
2 1/2 C. chopped coarsely pecans

Directions

1. Set your oven to 350 degrees F before doing anything else and grease and flour a 13x9-inch baking dish.
2. In a very large bowl, add the sugar and butter and beat until creamy.
3. Add eggs and beat until well combined.
4. Add the chocolate, vanilla and milk and beat until well combined.
5. In another bowl, mix together the flour, baking powder and salt.
6. Add the flour mixture into chocolate mixture and mix until just combined.
7. Fold in the dates and pecans.
8. Place the mixture into the prepared baking dish evenly.
9. Cook in the oven for about 80 minutes or till a toothpick inserted in the center comes out clean.
10. Remove from the oven and keep onto the wire rack to cool in the pan for about 10 minutes.
11. Carefully, invert the cake onto the wire rack to cool completely before serving.

BANANA
& Blueberry Split

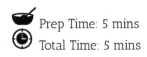 Prep Time: 5 mins
Total Time: 5 mins

Servings per Recipe: 1
Calories	1021.3
Fat	18.7g
Cholesterol	60.5mg
Sodium	189.3mg
Carbohydrates	212.1g
Protein	5.7g

Ingredients

3/4 C. blueberry jam
1 C. whipped cream
1 banana, ripe and split in half
lengthwise

1/3 C. chocolate ice cream
shredded coconut

Directions

1. In a small bowl, add the blueberry jam and enough water to thin and mix well.
2. In a banana split dish, spread whipped cream and drizzle with blueberry sauce.
3. Place banana halves on top of blueberry sauce, followed by the chocolate ice cream and shredded coconut.
4. Serve with a dollop of whipped cream.

Sun-Dried
Mushroom Pie

🥣 Prep Time: 20 mins
🕐 Total Time: 1 hr 5 mins

Servings per Recipe: 6
Calories	444.9
Fat	29.0g
Cholesterol	171.3mg
Sodium	744.6mg
Carbohydrates	27.1g
Protein	19.6g

Ingredients

18 inches pie crusts
1 (6 oz.) jars marinated artichoke hearts,
chopped
1/2 lb. mushroom, chopped
2 garlic cloves, minced
1 tbsp sun-dried tomato, minced

4 eggs
2 C. provolone cheese, shredded
1/8 tsp cayenne

Directions

1. Set your oven to 400 degrees F before doing anything else.
2. Reserve 1 unbaked pie shell.
3. Place the second crust onto a lightly floured surface and roll into 11-inch circle.
4. In a large frying pan, add the marinated artichoke hearts, mushrooms and garlic over medium heat and cook for about 2-3 minutes.
5. Stir in sun dried tomatoes and remove from the heat.
6. In a large bowl, add the eggs and beat lightly.
7. Stir in the cheese, cayenne and artichoke mixture.
8. Place the mixture into reserved pie shell.
9. Cover with rolled shell and crimp edges to seal the filling.
10. With a sharp knife, make four slits in the center of the top shell.
11. Cook in the oven for about 40-45 minutes.

VENTURA
Vegetarian Pate

Prep Time: 5 mins
Total Time: 5 mins

Servings per Recipe: 4
Calories	382.1
Fat	33.8g
Cholesterol	243.6mg
Sodium	119.9mg
Carbohydrates	12.4g
Protein	10.4g

Ingredients

2 large ripe avocados
1 tbsp chopped green onion
4 hard-boiled eggs
of fresh mint
chopped ground pepper
2 tbsp lemon juice
salt

1 1/4 C. sour cream
2 garlic cloves, crushed
2 tsp chopped olives
1 1/8 tsp sweet parsley
paprika

Directions

1. Cut the avocados in half and remove the seeds
2. Carefully, scoop out flesh and transfer into a bowl.
3. Reserve the avocado skins for serving.
4. In the bowl of avocado flesh, add the remaining ingredients and mash well.
5. Place the mixture into shells and serve.

Honey
Cheese Spread

🥣 Prep Time: 5 mins
🕐 Total Time: 5 mins

Servings per Recipe: 2
Calories	297.6
Fat	24.9g
Cholesterol	64.5mg
Sodium	176.0mg
Carbohydrates	13.3g
Protein	6.7g

Ingredients

4 oz. cream cheese
2 tbsp milk
3 tsp honey
3/4 tsp vanilla
1/16 tsp nutmeg
1/16 tsp cinnamon

3 tsp lemon juice
2 tbsp diced toasted almonds

Directions

1. In a bowl, add all the ingredients except almonds and mix until well combined.
2. Refrigerate to chill before serving.
3. Serve with a topping of the almonds.

GOLDEN STATE
Jell-O

Prep Time: 20 mins
Total Time: 2 hrs 20 mins

Servings per Recipe: 8

Calories	442.5
Fat	31.4g
Cholesterol	111.1mg
Sodium	297.6mg
Carbohydrates	32.3g
Protein	10.2g

Ingredients

2 (3 oz.) packaged lemon gelatin
1 (20 oz.) cans crushed pineapple
2 C. shredded cheddar cheese
1 pint heavy whipping cream

Directions

1. In a bowl, dissolve the Jell-O in 1 3/4 C. boiling water.
2. Add 15 ice cubes and stir until dissolved.
3. Refrigerate until "soft set".
4. Strain the pineapple partially and place into the bowl of Jell-O.
5. Add the Cheddar Cheese and stir to combine.
6. In another bowl, add the whipping cream and beat until soft peaks form.
7. Fold the whipped cream into Jell-O mixture.
8. Refrigerate for about 2 hours before serving.

American
Ground Beef Casserole

🥣 Prep Time: 15 mins
🕐 Total Time: 1 hr

Servings per Recipe: 6
Calories	348.9
Fat	18.6g
Cholesterol	83.9mg
Sodium	700.9mg
Carbohydrates	19.9g
Protein	25.3g

Ingredients

1 lb. lean ground beef
1/2 lb. sliced American cheese
2 C. chopped celery
1/2 C. chopped onion
1 (2 1/4 oz.) cans sliced ripe olives

2 C. fine egg noodles, crushed
1 (1 lb.) can tomato with juice

Directions

1. Set your oven to 350 degrees F before doing anything else.
2. Heat a skillet over medium heat and cook the ground beef until browned and mixture is crumbly.
3. Cut the canned tomatoes into small chunks, reserving juice.
4. Transfer the browned meat into a 2-quart shallow baking dish and top with cheese slices evenly, followed by celery, onion, olives, crushed noodles and tomato chunks.
5. Pour the reserved tomato juice on top evenly.
6. Cover the baking dish and cook in the oven for about 45 minutes.

PASTA SALAD
California

Prep Time: 15 mins
Total Time: 15 mins

Servings per Recipe: 6
Calories	268.9
Fat	7.8g
Cholesterol	3.2mg
Sodium	163.5mg
Carbohydrates	40.2g
Protein	10.2g

Ingredients

3 C. shelled pasta, uncooked
3 C. frozen broccoli
1/2 C. chopped yellow sweet pepper
3 tbsp margarine
5 garlic cloves, sliced

1/4 tsp crushed dried red pepper flakes
1/3 C. grated Parmigiano-Reggiano cheese

Directions

1. In a pan of salted boiling water, cook pasta according to package's directions.
2. In the last 2 minutes of cooking, stir in broccoli and sweet pepper.
3. Drain pasta and vegetables.
4. In a non-stick skillet, melt margarine over medium heat and sauté the garlic and dried red pepper flakes for about 1 minute.
5. In a large bowl, add pasta, vegetables, garlic mixture and salt and toss to coat well.
6. Serve with a sprinkling of the cheese.

Los Angeles
Monterey Quiche

🥣 Prep Time: 20 mins
🕐 Total Time: 55 mins

Servings per Recipe: 6
Calories	332.1
Fat	24.9g
Cholesterol	145.8mg
Sodium	340.2mg
Carbohydrates	14.7g
Protein	12.5g

Ingredients

1 ready-made pie crust
1 tbsp cooking oil
1/4 C. onion, chopped
1 clove garlic, crushed
1/2 C. red bell pepper , chopped
1/2 C. green bell pepper, chopped
1 1/2 C. Monterey jack cheese

3 large eggs
1 C. half-and-half milk
1/2 tsp dried basil

Directions

1. Set your oven to 425 degrees F before doing anything else.
2. Place a pie crust into 9-inch pie plate and gently, press to fit.
3. Cook in the oven for about 8 minutes.
4. For the filling: in a 10-inch skillet, heat oil and sauté the onion and garlic for about 1 minute.
5. Add the peppers and cook for about 2-3 minutes.
6. Place the peppers mixture over cooked pie crust and sprinkle with cheese.
7. In a small bowl, add half-and-half, eggs and basil and beat until well combined.
8. Carefully pour egg mixture over pepper mixture evenly.
9. Cook in the oven for about 15 minutes.
10. Now, set the oven to 350 degrees F and cook the quiche for about 20 minutes.

Made in the USA
Las Vegas, NV
09 January 2022

40207211R00052